The Reformation under Edward VI

The Reformation under Edward VI

A. F. Pollard

WIPF & STOCK · Eugene, Oregon

Wipf and Stock Publishers
199 W 8th Ave, Suite 3
Eugene, OR 97401

The Reformation under Edward VI
By Pollard, A. F.
ISBN 13: 978-1-5326-1610-5
Publication date 2/1/2017
Previously published by Cambridge University Press, 1934

THE REFORMATION UNDER EDWARD VI.

"WOE unto thee, O land," said the Preacher, "when thy king is a child." The truth of his words did not recommend them to the Parliament of Edward VI; and, when Dr John Story quoted them in his protest against the first Act of Uniformity, he was sent to expiate his boldness in the Tower. Yet he had all the precedents in English history on his side. Disaster and civil strife had attended the nonage of Henry III and Edward III, of Richard II and Henry VI; and the evils inseparable from the rule of a child had culminated in the murder of Edward V. When, in 1547, a sixth Edward ascended the throne, the signs were few of a break in the uniform ill-fortune of royal minorities. Abroad, Paul III was scheming to recover the allegiance of the schismatic realm; the Emperor was slowly crushing England's natural allies in Germany; France was watching her opportunity to seize Boulogne; and England herself was committed to a hazardous design on Scotland. At home, there was a religious revolution half-accomplished and a social revolution in ferment; evicted tenants and ejected monks infested the land, centres of disorder and raw material for revolt; the treasury was empty, the kingdom in debt, the coinage debased. In place of the old nobility of blood stood a new peerage raised on the ruins and debauched by the spoils of the Church, and created to be docile tools in the work of revolution. The royal authority, having undermined every other support of the political fabric, now passed to a Council torn by rival ambitions and conflicting creeds, robbed of royal prestige, and unbridled by the heavy hand that had taught it to serve but not to direct.

Henry VIII died at Whitehall in the early morning of Friday, January 28, 1547. Through the night his brother-in-law, the Earl of Hertford, and his secretary, Sir William Paget, had discussed in the gallery of the palace arrangements for the coming reign. Hertford then started to bring his nephew, the young King, from Hatfield, while Henry's death remained a secret. It was announced to Parliament and Edward was proclaimed early on the following Monday morning. In the afternoon he arrived in London, and an hour or so later the

Council met in the Tower. Its composition had been determined on St Stephen's Day, five weeks before, when Henry, acting on an authority specially granted him by Parliament, had drawn up a will, the genuineness of which was not disputed until the possibility of a Stewart succession drew attention to the obstacles it placed in their way to the throne. But the arrangements made in the will for the regency destroyed the balance of parties existing in Henry's later years. Norfolk had been sent to the Tower, and from the sixteen executors, who were to constitute Edward's Privy Council, Bishops Gardiner and Thirlby were expressly excluded. To the eleven, who had previously been of Henry's Council, five were added; two were the Chief Justices, Montagu and Bromley, but the other three, Denny, Herbert, and North, were all inclined towards religious change. Besides the sixteen executors Henry nominated twelve assistants, who were only to be called in when the others thought fit. Unless, in defiance of the testimony of those present when Henry drew up his will, that selection is to be regarded as due to the intrigues of the Reformers, it would seem that Henry deliberately sought to smooth the way for the Reformation by handing over the government to a Council committed to its principles. Not half a dozen of its members could be trusted to offer the least resistance to religious change; and, when the Council assembled in the Tower on that Monday afternoon, it only met to register a foregone conclusion.

Henry had been given no authority to nominate a Protector; but such a step was in accord with precedent and with general expectation, and one at least of the few conservatives on the Council thought that the appointment of Hertford to the protectorate afforded the best guarantee for the good government and security of the realm. He was uncle to the King, a successful general, and a popular favourite; and, though his peerage was but ten years old, it was older than any other that the Council could boast. He was to act only on the advice of his co-executors; but there was apparently no opposition to his appointment as Protector of the realm and Governor of the King's person. On the following day the young King and the peers gave their assent. Five days later Paget produced a list of promotions in the peerage which he said Henry had intended to make. Hertford became Duke of Somerset, and Lord High Treasurer and Earl Marshal in succession to Norfolk; Lisle became Earl of Warwick, and Wriothesley Earl of Southampton; Essex was made Marquis of Northampton, and baronies were conferred on Sir Thomas Seymour, Rich, and Sheffield.

Half of Henry's alleged intentions were not fulfilled, a strong argument in favour of their genuineness; Russell and St John had to wait for their promised earldoms, and seven others for their baronies, nor would Paget have then selected Wriothesley for promotion. For scarcely was Edward crowned (February 20) and Henry buried, when the Lord-Chancellor fell from power. He had been peculiarly identified with the reactionary policy of Henry's later years; and his ambition and ability inspired his colleagues with a distrust which increased when it was found that, in order to devote more time to politics, he had, without obtaining a warrant from the Council, issued a commission for the transaction of Chancery business during his absence. A complaint was at once lodged by the common lawyers, ever jealous of the Chancery side, and the judges unanimously declared that Southampton had forfeited the Chancellorship.

A more important change ensued. Doubts of the validity of a dead King's commission had already led the Chancellor to seek reappointment at the hands of his living sovereign, and the rest of the Council now followed suit. On March 13 Edward VI nominated a new Council of twenty-six. It consisted of the sixteen executors, except Somerset and Southampton, and the twelve assistants named by Henry VIII, but they now held office, not in virtue of their appointment by Henry's will, but of their commission from the boy-King. At the same time the Protector received a fresh commission. He was no longer bound to act by the advice of his colleagues; he was empowered to summon such councillors as he thought convenient, and to add to their numbers at will. No longer the first among equals, he became King in everything but name and prestige; and the attempt of Henry VIII to regulate the government after his death had, like that of every King before him, completely broken down.

Few rulers of England have been more remarkable than the Protector into whose hands thus passed the despotic power of the Tudors. Many have been more successful, many more skilled in the arts of government; but it is doubtful whether any have seen further into the future, or have been more strongly possessed of ideas which they have been unable to carry out. He was born before his time, a seer of visions and a dreamer of dreams. He dreamt of the union of England and Scotland, each retaining its local autonomy, as one empire of Great Britain, "having the sea for a wall, mutual love for a defence, and no need in peace to be ashamed or in war to be afraid of any worldly power." Running himself the universal race for wealth, he yet held it to be his special office and duty to hear poor men's complaints, to redress their wrongs, and to relieve their oppression. He strove to stay the economic revolution which was accumulating vast estates in the hands of the few, and turning the many into landless labourers or homeless vagrants; but his only success was an Act of Parliament whereby he gave his tenants legal security against eviction by himself. Bred in an arbitrary Court and entrusted with despotic power, he cast aside the weapons wherewith the Tudors worked their will and sought to govern on a basis of civil liberty and religious toleration. He abstained from interference in elections to Parliament or in its freedom of debate, and from all attempts to pack or intimidate juries. He believed that the strength of a King lay not in the severity of his laws or the rigour of his penalties, but in the affections of his people; and not one instance of death or torture for religion stains the brief and troubled annals of his rule.

The absolutism, which came in with the new monarchy and was perfected by Cromwell, was relaxed; and the first Parliament summoned by the Protector (November 4, 1547) effected a complete revolution in the spirit of the laws. Nearly all the treasons created since 1352 were swept away, and many of the felonies. It was, indeed, still treason to deny the Royal Supremacy by writing, printing, overt deed or act; but it was no longer treason to do so by "open preaching, express words or sayings." Benefit of clergy and right of sanctuary were restored; wives of attainted persons were permitted to recover their dower; accusations of treason were to be preferred within thirty days of the offence; no one was to be condemned unless he confessed or was accused by two sufficient and lawful witnesses; and Proclamations were no longer to have the force of law. The heresy laws, the Act of Six Articles, all the prohibitions against printing the Scriptures in English, against reading, preaching, teaching, or expounding the Scriptures, "and all and every other act or acts of Parliament concerning doctrine or matters of religion" were erased from the Statute-book.

The main result of this new-found liberty was to give fresh impetus to the Reformation in England. The Act of Six Articles, with all its ferocious penalties, had failed to cure diversities of opinion; and the controversies of which Henry complained to his Parliament in 1545 now broke out with redoubled fury. Among a people unused to freedom and inflamed by religious passions, liberty naturally degenerated into licence. The tongues of the divines were loosed; and they filled the land with a Babel of voices. Each did what was right in his own eyes, and every parish church became the scene of religious experiment. Exiles from abroad flocked to partake in the work and to propagate the doctrines they had imbibed at their respective Meccas. Some came from Lutheran cities in Germany, some from Geneva, and some from Zwinglian Zurich. In their path followed a host of foreign divines, some invited by Cranmer to form a sort of ecumenical council for the purification of the Anglican Church, some fleeing from the wrath of Charles V or from the perils of civil war. From Strassburg came in 1547 Pietro Martire Vermigli, better known as Peter Martyr, a native of Florence and an ex-Augustinian, and Emmanuel Tremellius the Hebraist, a Jew of Ferrara; and from Augsburg came Bernardino Ochino, a native of Siena, once a Franciscan and then a Capuchin. In 1548 John à Lasco (Laski), a Polish noble, and his disciple, John Utenhove, a native of Ghent, followed from Emden; and in 1549 Martin Bucer and Paul Fagius fled hither from Strassburg. Jean Véron, a Frenchman from Sens, had been in England eleven years, but celebrated the era of liberty by publishing in 1547 a violent attack on the Mass. Most of these were Zwinglians; and even among the Lutherans many soon inclined towards the doctrine of the Swiss Reformers. Of the humbler immigrants who came to teach or to trade, not a few were Anabaptists, Socinians, and heretics of every hue; and England became, in the words of one horrified politician, the harbour for all infidelity.

The clamour raised by the advent of this foreign legion has somewhat obscured the comparative insignificance of its influence on the development of the English Church. The continental Reformers came too late to affect the moderate changes introduced during Somerset's protectorate, and even the Second Prayer-book of Edward VI owed less to their persuasions than has often been supposed. England never became Lutheran, Zwinglian, or Calvinistic; and she would have resented dictation from Wittenberg, Zurich, or Geneva as keenly as she did from Rome, had the authority of Luther, Zwingli, or Calvin ever attained the proportions of that of the Roman Pontiff. Each indeed had his adherents in England, but their influence was never more than sectional, and failed to turn the course of the English Reformation into any foreign channel.

In so far as the English Reformers sought spiritual inspiration from other than primitive sources, it is probable, although the point is not capable of complete demonstration, that they, consciously or unconsciously, derived this inspiration from Wiclif. Like them, he appealed to the State to remedy abuses in the Church, attacked ecclesiastical endowments, and gradually receded from the Catholic doctrine of the Mass. The Reformation in England was divergent in origin, method, and aim from all the phases of the movement abroad; it left the English Church without a counterpart in Europe, —so insular in character that no subsequent attempt at union with any foreign Church has ever come within measurable distance of success. It was in its main aspect practical and not doctrinal; it concerned itself less with dogma than with conduct, and its favourite author was Erasmus, not because he preached any distinctive theology, but because he lashed the evil practices of the Church. Englishmen are little subject to the bondage of logic or abstract ideas, and they began their Reformation, not with the enunciation of any new truth, but with an attack upon the clerical exaction of excessive probate dues. No dogma played in England the part that Predestination or Justification by Faith played in Europe. There arose a master of prophetic invective in Latimer and a master of liturgies in Cranmer, but no one meet to be compared with the great religious thinkers of the world. Hence the influence of English Reformers on foreign Churches was even less than that of foreign divines in England. Anglicans never sought to proselytise other Christian Churches, nor England to wage other than defensive wars of religion; in Ireland and Scotland, which appear to afford exceptions, the religious motive was always subordinate to a political end.

The Reformation in England was mainly a domestic affair, a national protest against national grievances rather than part of a cosmopolitan movement towards doctrinal change. It originated in political exigencies, local and not universal in import; and was the work of Kings and statesmen, whose minds were absorbed in national problems, rather than of divines whose faces were set towards the purification of the universal Church. It was an ecclesiastical counterpart of the growth of nationalities at the expense of the medieval ideal of the unity of the civilised world. Its effect was to make the Church in England the Church of England, a national Church, recognising as its head the English King, using in its services the English tongue, limited in its jurisdiction to the English Courts, and fenced about with a uniformity imposed by the English legislature. This nationalisation of the Church had one other effect: it brought to a sudden end the medieval struggle between Church and State. The Church had only been enabled to wage that conflict on equal terms by the support it received as an integral part of the visible Church on earth; and when that support was withdrawn it sank at once into a position of dependence upon the State. From the time of the submission of the clergy to Henry VIII there has been no instance of the English Church successfully challenging the supreme authority of the State.

It was mainly on these lines, laid down by Henry VIII, that the Reformation continued under Edward VI. The papal jurisdiction was no more; the use of English had been partially introduced into the services of the Church; the Scriptures had been translated; steps had been taken in the direction of uniformity, doctrinal and liturgical; and something had been done to remove medieval accretions, such as the worship of images, and to restore religion to what Reformers considered its primitive purity. That Henry intended his so-called "settlement" to be final is an assumption at variance with some of the evidence; for he had entrusted his son's education exclusively to men of the New Learning, he had given the same party an overwhelming preponderance in the Council of Regency, and according to Cranmer he was bent in the last few months of his life upon a scheme for pulling down roods, suppressing the ringing of bells and turning the Mass into a Communion. Cranmer himself had for some years been engaged upon a reform of the Church services which developed into the First Book of Common Prayer, and the real break in religious policy came, not at the accession of Edward VI, but after the fall of Somerset and the expulsion of the Catholics from the Council. The statute procured by Henry VIII from Parliament, which enabled his son, on coming of age, to annul all Acts passed during his minority, was probably due to an overweening sense of the importance of the kingly office; but, although it was repealed in Edward's first year, it inevitably strengthened the natural doubts of the competence of the Council to exercise an ecclesiastical supremacy vested in the King. No government, however, could afford to countenance such a suicidal theory; and the Council had constitutional right on its side when it insisted that the authority of the King, whether in ecclesiastical or civil matters, was the same whatever his age might be, and refused to consider the minority as a bar to further prosecution of the Reformation.

No doubt, they were led in the same direction, some by conviction and some by the desire, as Sir William Petre expressed it, "to fish again in the tempestuous seas of this world for gain and wicked mammon." But there was also popular pressure behind them. Zeal and energy, if not numbers, were on the side of religious change, and the Council found it necessary to restrain rather than stimulate the ardour of the Reformers. One of its first acts was to bind over the wardens and curate of St Martin's, Ironmonger Lane, to restore images which they had "contrary to the King's doctrine and order" removed from their church. Six months later the Council was only prevented from directing a general replacement of images illegally destroyed by a fear of the controversy such a step would arouse; and it had no hesitation in punishing the destroyers. In November, 1547, it sought by Proclamation to stay the rough treatment which priests suffered at the hands of London serving-men and apprentices, and sent round commissioners to take an inventory of church goods in order to prevent the extensive embezzlement practised by local magnates. Early in the following year Proclamations were issued denouncing unauthorised innovations, silencing preachers who urged them, and prohibiting flesh-eating in Lent. In April, 1548, the ecclesiastical authorities were straitly charged to take legal proceedings against those who, encouraged by the lax views prevalent on marriage, were guilty of such "insolent and unlawful acts" as putting away one wife and marrying another. The Marquis of Northampton was himself summoned before the Council and summarily ordered to separate from the lady he called his second wife. Similarly the first Statute of the reign was directed not against the Catholics, but against reckless Reformers; it sought to restrain all who impugned or spoke unreverently of the Sacrament of the altar; the right of the clergy to tithe was reaffirmed, and the Canon Law as to precontracts and sanctuary, abolished by Henry VIII, was restored. It was no wonder that the clergy thought the moment opportune for the recovery of their position as an Estate of the realm, and petitioned that ecclesiastical laws should be submitted to their approval, or that they should be readmitted to their lost representation in the House of Commons.

These measures illustrate alike the practical conservatism of Somerset's government and the impracticability of the theoretical toleration to which he inclined. His dislike of coercion occasionally got the better of his regard for his own proclamations, as when he released Thomas Hancock from his sureties taken for unlicensed preaching. But he soon realised that the government could not abdicate its ecclesiastical functions, least of all in the early days of the Royal Supremacy, when the Bishops and Cranmer especially looked to the State for guidance. Personally he leaned to the New Learning, and, like most Englishmen, he was Erastian in his view of the relations between Church and State and somewhat prejudiced against sacerdotalism. Yet, in spite of the fact that after his death he was regarded as a martyr by the French Reformed Church, he cannot any more than the English Reformation be labelled Lutheran, Zwinglian, or Calvinist; and, when he found it incumbent upon him to take some line in ecclesiastical politics, he chose one of comparative moderation and probably the line of least resistance. The Royal Supremacy was perhaps somewhat nakedly asserted when, at the commencement of the reign, Bishops renewed their commissions to exercise spiritual jurisdiction, and when in the first session of Parliament the form of episcopal election was exchanged for direct nomination by royal letters patent. But the former practice had been enforced, and the latter suggested, in the reign of Henry VIII, and Somerset secured a great deal more episcopal co-operation than did either Northumberland or Elizabeth. Convocation demanded, unanimously in one case and by a large majority in the other, the administration of the Sacrament in both kinds and liberty for the clergy to marry; and a majority of the Bishops in the House of Lords voted for all the ecclesiastical bills passed during his protectorate. Only Gardiner and Bonner offered any resistance to the Visitation of 1547; and it must be concluded, either that Somerset's religious changes accorded with the preponderant clerical opinion, or that clerical subservience surpassed the compliance of laymen.

The responsibility for these changes cannot be apportioned with any exactness. Probably Gardiner was not far from the mark, when he implied that Cranmer and not the Protector was the innovating spirit; and the comparative caution with which the Reformers at first proceeded was as much due to Somerset's restraining influence as the violence of their later course was to the simulated zeal of Warwick. Cranmer's influence with the Council was greater than it had been with Henry VIII; to him it was left to work out the details of the movement, and the first step taken in the new reign was the Archbishop's issue of the Book of Homilies for which he had failed to obtain the sanction of King and Convocation five years before. Their main features were a comparative neglect of the Sacraments and the exclusion of charity as a means of salvation. Gardiner attacked the Book on these grounds; and, possibly out of deference to his protest, the saving power of charity was affirmed in the Council's injunctions to the royal visitors a few months later.

The Homilies were followed by Nicholas Udall's edition of the Paraphrase of Erasmus that had been prepared under Henry VIII, and was now intended, partly no doubt as a solvent of old ideas, but partly as a corrective of the extreme Protestant versions of Tyndall and Coverdale, which, now that Henry's prohibition was relaxed, recovered their vogue. The substitution of English for Latin in the services of the Church was gradually carried out in the Chapel Royal as an example to the rest of the kingdom. Compline was sung in English on Easter Monday, 1547; the sermon was preached, and the *Te Deum* sung, in English on September 18 to celebrate Pinkie; and at the opening of Parliament on November 4, the *Gloria in Excelsis*, the Creed, and the *Agnus* were all sung in English. Simultaneously, Sternhold, a gentleman of the Court, was composing his metrical version of the Psalms in English, which was designed to supplant the "lewd" ballads of the people and in fact eventually made "psalm-singing" a characteristic of advanced ecclesiastical Reformers.

The general Visitation in the summer and autumn of 1547 was mainly concerned with reforming practical abuses, with attempts to compel the wider use of English in services, the removal of images that were abused, and a full recognition of the Supremacy of the boy-King. In November and December Convocation recommended the administration of the Sacrament in both kinds, and liberty for priests to marry; but the latter change did not receive parliamentary sanction until the following year. The bill against "unreverent" speaking of the Sacrament was, by skilful parliamentary strategy which seems to have been due to Somerset, combined with one for its administration in both kinds, the motive being obviously to induce Catholics to vote for it for the sake of the first part, and Reformers for the sake of the second. The Chantries Bill was in the main a renewal of the Act of 1545; but its object was now declared to be the endowment of education, and not the defence of the realm; and the reason alleged for suppression was the encouragement that chantries gave to superstition and not their appropriation by private persons. Such opposition as this bill encountered was due less to theological objections than to the reluctance of corporations to surrender any part of their revenues; and Gardiner subsequently expressed his concurrence in the measure. Its effect on gilds was to convert such of their revenues as had previously been devoted to obits and masses into a rent paid to the Crown; but a bill, which was introduced a year later and passed the House of Commons, to carry out the intentions of founding schools alleged in the Chantries Act, disappeared after its first reading in the House of Lords on February 18, 1549.

Immediately after the prorogation in January, 1548, questions were addressed to the Bishops as to the best form of Communion service; the answers varied, some being in favour of the exclusive use of English, some of the exclusive use of Latin. The form actually adopted approaches most nearly to Tunstall's recommendation, a compromise whereby Latin was retained for the essential part of the Mass, while certain prayers in English were adopted. This new Order for Communion was issued in March, 1548, a Proclamation ordering its use after Easter was prefixed, and in a rubric all "varying of any rite or ceremony in the Mass" was forbidden. A more decided innovation was made in February, when by Proclamation the Council ordered the removal of all images, under the impression that this drastic measure would cause less disturbance than the widespread contentions as to whether the images were abused or not. Ashes and palms and candles on Candlemas Day had been forbidden in January; and soon afterwards a Proclamation was issued against the practice of creeping to the cross on Good Friday and the use of holy bread and holy water. These prohibitions had been contemplated under Henry VIII; they met with guarded approval from Gardiner; and they were comparatively slight concessions to the Reformers in a Proclamation, the main purpose of which was to check unauthorised innovations. The Council also sought to remove a fruitful cause of tumult by forbidding the clergy to preach outside their own cures without a special licence. How far this bore hardly on the Catholics depends upon the proportion of Catholics to Reformers among the beneficed clergy; but it is fairly obvious that it was directed against the two extremes, the ejected monks on the one hand and the itinerant "hot-gospellers" on the other.

These measures were temporary expedients designed to preserve some sort of quiet, pending the production of the one "uniform and godly" order of service towards which the Church had been moving ever since the break with Rome. The assertion of the national character of the English Church necessarily involved an attempt at uniformity in its services. The legislation of 1547 seemed to imply unlimited religious liberty, and to leave the settlement of religious controversy to public discussion; but it was not possible to carry out a reformation solely by means of discussion. Local option, too, was alien to the centralising government of the Tudors and, unchecked, might well have precipitated a Thirty Years' War in England. Uniformity, however, was not the end which the government had in view, so much as the means to ensure peace and quietness. Somerset was less anxious to obliterate the liturgical variations between one parish and another, than to check the contention between Catholics and Reformers which made every parish the scene of disorder and strife; and the only way he perceived of effecting this object was to draw up one uniform order, a compromise and a standard which all might be persuaded or compelled to observe. Nor was the idea of uniformity a novel one. There were various Uses in medieval England, those of York, Hereford, Lincoln, and Sarum; but the divergence between these forms of service was slight, and before the Reformation the Sarum Use seems to have prevailed over the greater part of the kingdom.

As regards doctrine, the several formularies issued by Henry VIII accustomed men to the idea that the teaching of the Church of England should be uniform and something different from that of either Catholic or Reformed Churches on the Continent. Nor was it only in the eyes of antipapalists that some reformation of Church service books seemed necessary. The reformed Breviary of Cardinal Quignon, dedicated in 1535 to Paul III, anticipated many of the changes which Cranmer made in the ancient Use. In Catholic as well as in Protestant churches the medieval services were simplified and shortened, partly in view of the busier life of the sixteenth century, and partly to allow more time for preaching and reading the Scriptures.

Thus Cranmer was only following the general tendency when, in 1543, he obtained Henry's consent to the examination and reformation of the Church service books. For some years he laboured at this task; but what stage he had reached in 1547 when Convocation demanded the production of his work is not clear. That demand was refused; and it was not until September, 1548, that the final stage in the evolution of the First Book of Common Prayer was commenced. Its development remains shrouded in obscurity. There is no trace of any formal commission to execute the task, of the composition of the revising body, or of the place where it carried on its work. Cranmer without doubt took the principal part, and once at least he called other divines to help him at Windsor; but it is unsafe to assume that the revisers continued to sit there, or indeed that there was any definite body of revisers at all. Probably about the end of October most of the Bishops were invited to subscribe to the completed book; but it seems to have undergone further alteration without their consent, and there is not sufficient evidence to show that it was submitted to Convocation. In December, it was in the House of Lords the subject of an animated debate in which Cranmer, Ridley, and Sir Thomas Smith defended, and Tunstall, Bonner, Thirlby, and Heath attacked, the way in which it treated the doctrine of the Mass.

Cranmer himself had already advanced beyond the point of view adopted in the First Book of Common Prayer. In the autumn of 1548 Bullinger's correspondents had rejoiced over the Archbishop's abandonment of Lutheran views; but the doctrine assumed, if not affirmed, in the new Book seemed to them to constitute "a marvellous recantation." The First Book of Common Prayer bore, indeed, little resemblance to the service-books of the Zwinglian and Calvinistic Churches. Its affinity with Lutheran liturgies was more marked, because the Anglican and Lutheran revisers made the ancient uses of the Church their groundwork, while the other Reformed churches sought to obliterate as far as possible all traces of the Mass. It is the most conservative of all the liturgies of the Reformation; its authors wished to build upon, and not to destroy, the past; and the materials on which they worked were almost exclusively the Sarum Use and the Breviary of Cardinal Quignon. Whatever intention they may have had of denying the supplemental character of the sacrifice of the Mass was studiously veiled by the retention of Roman terminology in a somewhat equivocal sense; room was to be made, if possible, for both interpretations; the sacrifice might be regarded as real and absolute, or merely as commemorative and analogical. The "abominable canon" was transformed because it shut the door on all but the Roman doctrine of the Mass, and the design of the government was to open the door to the New Learning without definitely closing it on the Old.

The intention was to make the uniform order tolerable to as many as was possible, and the result was a cautious and tentative compromise, a sort of Anglican *Interim*, which was more successful than its German counterpart. The penalties attached to its non-observance by the First Act of Uniformity were milder than those imposed by any of the subsequent Acts, and they were limited to the clergy. Neither in the First Act of Uniformity nor in the First Book of Common Prayer is there any attempt to impose a doctrinal test or dogmatic unity. All that was enforced was a uniformity of service; and even here considerable latitude was allowed in details like vestments and ritual. A few months later a licensed preacher declared at St Paul's, that faith was not to be "coacted," but that every man might believe as he would. Doctrinal unity was in fact incompatible with that appeal to private judgment which was the essence of the Reformation, and Somerset's government was wise in limiting its efforts to securing an outward and limited uniformity.

Even this was sufficiently difficult. Eager Reformers began at once to agitate for the removal of those parts of the Book of Common Prayer which earned Gardiner's commendation, while Catholics resented its departure from the standard of orthodoxy set up by the Six Articles. Religious liberty was in itself distasteful to the majority; and zealots on either side were less angered by the persecution of themselves than by the toleration of their enemies. Dislike of the new service book was keenest in the west, where the men of Cornwall spoke no English and could not understand an English service book; they knew little Latin, but they were accustomed to the phrases of the ancient Use, and men tolerate the incomprehensible more easily than the unfamiliar. So they rose in July, 1549, and demanded the restoration of the old service, the old ceremonies, the old images, and the ancient monastic endowments. They asked that the Sacrament should be administered to laymen in one kind and only at Easter—a strange demand in the mouths of those who maintained the supreme importance of the sacramental system—and that all who refused to worship it should suffer death as heretics; the Bibles were to be called in again, and Cardinal Pole was to be made first or second in the King's Council.

On the whole the Protector's religious policy was accompanied by singularly little persecution; and the instances quoted by Roman Catholic writers date almost without exception from the period after his fall. The Princess Mary flatly refused to obey the new law; and after some remonstrance Somerset granted her permission to hear Mass privately in her own house. Gardiner was more of an opportunist than Mary; probably he thought that his opposition would be the more effective for being less indiscriminate. But it was no less deliberate, and in the early and effective days of the Royal Supremacy, when Bishops were regarded as ecclesiastical sheriffs, their resistance to authority was as little tolerated as that of the soldier or the civil servant would be now. Gardiner was sent to the Fleet, but he was treated by Somerset with what was considered excessive lenience; and in January, 1548, he was, by the King's general pardon, released. He returned to his diocese, and preached obedience to the Council on the ground that to suffer evil was a Christian's duty. The reason was scarcely pleasing to the government, and on June 29 he was ordered to preach a sermon at Whitehall declaring the supreme ecclesiastical authority of the young King during his minority; at the same time he was forbidden to deal with the doctrines that were in dispute. On neither point did he give satisfaction, and on the following day he was sent to the Tower. Bonner was sent to the Marshalsea for a similar reason. He had protested against the visitation of 1547, but withdrew his protest, and after a few weeks in the Fleet remained at liberty until September, 1549. He was then accused of not enforcing the new Book of Common Prayer and was ordered to uphold the ecclesiastical authority of the King in a sermon at St Paul's; on his failure to do so he was imprisoned and deprived by Cranmer of his bishopric; and at the same time his chaplain Feckenham was sent to the Tower. These, however, are practically the only instances of religious persecution exercised during Somerset's protectorate.

This comparative moderation, while consonant with the Protector's own inclination, was also rendered advisable by the critical condition of England's relations with foreign powers. Any violent breach with Catholicism, any bitter persecution of its adherents, would have turned into open enmity the lukewarm friendship of Charles V, precipitated that hostile coalition of Catholic Europe for which the Pope and Cardinal Pole were intriguing, and rendered impossible the union with Scotland on which the Tudors had set their hearts. For this reason Somerset declined (March, 1547) the proffered alliance of the German Protestant Princes; and, to strengthen his position, he began negotiations for a treaty with France, and discussed the possibility of a marriage between the Princess Elizabeth and a member of the French royal family. The treaty was on the point of ratification when the death of Francis I (March 31) produced a revolution in French policy. The new King, Henry II, had, when Dauphin, proclaimed his intention of demanding the immediate retrocession of Boulogne; but his designs were not confined to the expulsion of the English from France. He also dreamt of a union with Scotland. Through Diane de Poitiers the Guise influence was strong at Paris; through Mary de Guise, the Queen Regent of Scotland, it was almost as powerful at Edinburgh; and England was menaced with a *pacte de famille* more threatening than that of the Bourbons two centuries later. Even Francis had considered a scheme for marrying the infant Queen of Scots to a French Prince; and, while Henry VIII in his last days had been organising a new invasion of Scotland, the French King had been equally busy with preparations for the defence of his ancient allies.

Henry II of France changed a defensive into an offensive policy; and, in taking up the Scottish policy urged upon him by Henry VIII, Somerset was seeking, not merely to carry out one of the most cherished of Tudor aims, but to ward off a danger which now presented itself in more menacing guise than ever before. There might be doubts as to the policy of pressing the union with Scotland at that juncture—there could be none as to the overwhelming and immediate necessity of preventing a union between Scotland and France; and Gardiner's advice, to let the Scots be Scots until the King of England came of age, would have been fatal unless he could guarantee a similar abstinence during the same period on the part of Henry II. Somerset, however, pursued methods different from those of Henry VIII. He abandoned alike the feudal claim to suzerainty over Scotland and the claim to sovereignty which Henry had asserted in 1542; he refrained from offensive references to James V as a "pretensed king"; he endeavoured to persuade the Scots that union was as much the interest of Scotland as of England; and all he required was the fulfilment of the treaty which the Scots themselves had made in 1543. His efforts were vain; encouraged by French aid in men, money, and ships, the Scottish government refused to negotiate, and stirred up trouble in Ireland. In September, 1547, the Protector crossed the border, and on the 10th he won the crushing victory of Pinkie Cleugh. The result was to place the Lowlands at England's mercy; and, thinking he had shown the futility of resistance, Somerset attempted to complete the work by conciliation.

During the winter he put forward some remarkable suggestions for the Union between England and Scotland. He proposed to abolish the names of English and Scots associated with centuries of strife, and to "take again the old indifferent name of Britons." The United Kingdom was to be known as the Empire, and its sovereign as the Emperor of Great Britain. There was to be no forfeiture of lands or of liberty, but freedom of trade and of marriage. Scotland was to retain her local autonomy, and the children of her Queen were to rule over England. Never in the history of the two realms had such liberal terms been offered, but reason, which might have counselled acceptance, was no match for pride, prejudice, and vested interests. Care was taken that these proposals should not reach the mass of the Scottish people. Most of the nobility were in receipt of French pensions; and the influence of the Church was energetically thrown into the scale against accommodation with a schismatic enemy. It was only among the peasantry, where Protestantism had made some way, that the Union with England was popular; and that influence was more than counterbalanced by the presence of French soldiery in the streets of Edinburgh and in most of the strongholds of Scotland. The seizure of Haddington in April, 1548, secured for a year the English control of the Lowlands; but it did not prevent the young Queen's transportation to France, where she was at once betrothed to the Dauphin. This step provoked Somerset in October to revive once more England's feudal claims over Scotland, and to hint that the English King had a voice in the marriage of his vassal. But the Guises could afford to laugh at threats, since they knew that the internal condition of England in 1549 prevented the threats being backed by adequate force in Scotland or in France. In both kingdoms they became more aggressive; they were in communication with rebels in Ireland, and in January, 1549, a French emissary was sent to England to see if Thomas Seymour's conspiracy might be fanned into civil war.

Thomas Seymour, the only one of the Protector's brothers who showed any aptitude or inclination for public life, had served with distinction on sea and land under Henry VIII. He had commanded a fleet in the Channel in 1545, had been made master of the Ordnance, and had wooed Catharine Parr before she became Henry's sixth wife. A few days before the end of the late reign he was sworn of the Privy Council; and on Edward's accession he was made Baron Seymour and Lord High Admiral. These dignities seemed to him poor compared with his brother's, and he thought he ought to be governor of the King's person. After unsuccessful attempts to secure the hands of the Princess Mary, the Princess Elizabeth, and Anne of Cleves, he married Catharine Parr without consulting his colleagues; and before her death he renewed his advances to the Princess Elizabeth. He refused the command of the fleet during the Pinkie campaign, and stayed at home to create a party for himself in the country. He suffered pirates to prey on the trade of the Channel, and himself received a share of their ill-gotten goods; he made a corrupt bargain with Sir William Sharington, who provided him with money by tampering with the Bristol mint, and he began to store arms and ammunition in various strongholds which he acquired for the purpose. The disclosure of Sharington's frauds (January, 1549) brought Seymour's plots to light. After many examinations, in which Warwick and Southampton took a leading part, a bill of attainder against the Admiral was introduced into Parliament; it passed, with a few dissentients, in the House of Commons, and unanimously in the House of Lords, and on March 20 Seymour was executed. The sentence was probably just, but the Protector paid dearly for his weakness in allowing it to be carried out. His enemies, such as Warwick and Southampton, who seem to have been the prime movers in Seymour's ruin, perceived more clearly than Somerset, how fatally his brother's death would undermine his own position and alienate popular favour in the struggle on which he had now embarked in the cause of the poor against the great majority of the Council and of the ruling classes in England.

This struggle was fought over the Protector's attitude towards the momentous social revolution of the sixteenth century, a movement which lay at the root of most of the internal difficulties of Tudor governments, and vitally affected the history of the reign of Edward VI. It was in effect the breaking up of the foundations upon which society had been based for five hundred years, the substitution of competition for custom as the regulating principle of the relations between the various classes of the community.

Social organisation in medieval times was essentially conservative; custom was the characteristic sanction to which appeal was universally made. Land, in the eyes of its military feudal lord, was valuable less as a source of money than as a source of men; it was not rent but service that he required, and he was seldom tempted to reduce his service-roll in order to swell his revenues. But the Black Death and the Peasants' Revolt, co-operating with more silent and gradual causes, weakened the mutual bonds of interest between landlord and tenant, while the extension of commerce produced a wealthy class which slowly gained admission into governing circles and established itself on the land. To these new landlords land was mainly an investment; they applied to it the principles they practised in trade; and sought to extract from it not men but money. They soon found that the *petite culture* of feudal times was not the most profitable use to which land could be turned; and they began the practice known as "engrossing," of which complaint was made as early as 1484 in the Lord Chancellor's speech to Parliament. Their method was to buy up several holdings, which they did not lease to so many yeomen, but consolidated, leaving the old homesteads to decay; the former tenants became either vagabonds or landless labourers, who boarded with their masters and were precluded by their position from marrying and raising families. Similarly the new landed gentry sought to turn their vague and disputed rights over common lands into palpable means of revenue. Sometimes with and often without the consent of the commoners, they proceeded to enclose vast stretches of land with a view to converting it either to tillage or to pasture. The latter proved to be the more remunerative, owing to the great development of the wool-market in the Netherlands; and it was calculated that the lord, who converted open arable land into enclosed pasture land, thereby doubled his income.

Yet another method of extracting the utmost monetary value from the land was the raising of rents; it had rarely occurred to the uncommercial feudal lord to interfere with the ancient service or rent which his tenants paid for their lands, but respect for immemorial custom counted for little against the retired trader's habit of demanding the highest price for his goods. The direct result of these tendencies was to pauperise a large section of the community, though the aggregate wealth of the whole was increased. The English yeomen, who had supplied the backbone of English armies and the great majority of students at English Universities, were depressed into vagabonds or hired labourers. As indirect results, schools and universities declined; and foreign mercenaries took the place of English soldiers; for "shepherds" wrote a contemporary "be but ill archers."

These evils had not passed without notice from statesmen and writers in the previous reign. Wolsey, inspired perhaps by Sir Thomas More, had in 1517 made a vigorous effort to check enclosures; and More himself had sympathetically pourtrayed the grievances of the population in the pages of his *Utopia*. Later in the reign of Henry VIII remedial measures had been warmly urged by conservatives like Thomas Lupset and Thomas Starkey, and by more radical thinkers like Brynkelow and Robert Crowley. But the King and his ministers were absorbed in the task of averting foreign complications and effecting a religious revolution, while courtiers and ordinary members of Parliament were not concerned to check a movement from which they reaped substantial profit. After the accession of Edward VI the constant aggravation of the evil and the sympathy it was known to evoke in high quarters brought the question more prominently forward. The Protector himself denounced with more warmth than prudence the misdeeds of new lords "sprung from the dunghill." Latimer inveighed against them in eloquent sermons preached at Court; Scory told the young King that his subjects had become "more like the slavery and peasantry of France than the ancient and godly yeomanry of England." Cranmer, Lever, and other reforming divines held similar opinions, but the most earnest and active member of the party, which came to be known as the "Commonwealth's men," was John Hales, whose *Discourse of the Common Weal* is one of the most informing documents of the age.

The existence of this party alarmed the official class, but the Protector more or less openly adopted its social programme; and it was doubtless with his connivance that various remedial measures were introduced into Parliament in December, 1547. One bill "for bringing up poor men's children" was apparently based on a suggestion made by Brynkelow in the previous reign that a certain number of the poorest children in each town should be brought up at the expense of the community; another bill sought to give farmers and lessees security of tenure; and a third provided against the decay of tillage and husbandry. None of these bills got beyond a second reading, and the only measure which found favour with Parliament was an Act which provided that a weekly collection in churches should be made for the impotent poor, and that confirmed vagabonds might be sold into slavery.

The failure of Parliament to find adequate remedies was the signal for agrarian disturbances in Hertfordshire and other counties in the spring of 1548; and the Protector, moved thereto by divers supplications, some of which are extant, now determined to take action independently of Parliament. On the first of June he issued a Proclamation, in which he referred to the "insatiable greediness" of those by whose means "houses were decayed, parishes diminished, the force of the realm weakened, and Christian people eaten up and devoured of brute beasts and driven from their houses by sheep and bullocks." Commissioners were appointed to enquire into the extent of enclosures made since 1485 and the failure of previous legislation to check them, and to make returns of those who broke the law.

The commissioners, of whom Hales was the chief, encountered an organised and stubborn resistance from those on whose conduct they were to report. With a view to disarming opposition, the presentment of offenders was postponed, until evidence should have been collected to form the basis of measures to be laid before Parliament; and subsequently Hales obtained from the Protector a general pardon of the offenders presented by the commission. Both measures failed to mollify the gentry, who resolutely set themselves to burke the enquiry. They packed the juries with their own servants; they threatened to evict tenants who gave evidence against them, and even had them indicted at the assizes. Other means taken to conceal the truth were the ploughing up of one furrow in a holding enclosed to pasture, the whole being then returned as arable land, and the placing of a couple of oxen with a flock of sheep and passing off the sheep-run as land devoted to fatting beasts. Under these circumstances it was with difficulty that the commissioners could get to work at all; and only those commissions on which Hales sat appear to have made any return. The opposition was next transferred to the Houses of Parliament. In November, 1548, Hales introduced various bills for maintaining tillage and husbandry, for restoring tenements which had been suffered to decay, and for checking the growth of sheep-farms. An Act was passed remitting the payment of fee-farms for three years in order that the proceeds might be devoted to finding work for the unemployed; and a tax of twopence was imposed on every sheep kept in pasture. But the more important bills were received with open hostility; and after acrimonious debates they were all rejected either by the Lords or by the Commons.

This result is not surprising, for the statute of 1430 had limited parliamentary representation, so far as the agricultural districts were concerned, to the landed gentry; and there are frequent complaints of the time that the representation of the boroughs had also fallen mainly into the hands of capitalists, who, by engrossing household property and monopolising trade, were providing the poorer townsfolk with grievances similar to those of the country folk. Nor was there a masterful Tudor to overawe resistance. The government was divided, for Somerset's adoption of the peasants' cause had driven the majority of the Council into secret opposition. Warwick seized the opportunity. Hitherto there had been no apparent differences between him and Somerset; but now his park was ploughed up as an illegal enclosure, and he fiercely attacked Hales as the cause of the agrarian discontent. Other members of the government, including even his ally Paget, remonstrated with the Protector, but without effect, except to stiffen his back and confirm him in his course. Fresh instructions were issued to the commissioners in 1549; and, having failed to obtain relief for the poor by legislation, Somerset resorted to the arbitrary expedient of erecting a sort of Court of Requests, which sat in his own house under Cecil's presidency to hear any complaint that poor suitors might bring against their oppressors.

Measures like these were of little avail to avert the dangers Somerset feared. Parliament had scarcely disposed of his bills, when the resentment of the peasants found vent in open revolt. The flame was kindled first in Somersetshire; thence it spread eastwards into Wilts and Gloucestershire, southwards into Dorset and Hampshire and northwards into Berks and the shires of Oxford and Buckingham. Surrey remained in a state of "quavering quiet"; but Kent felt the general impulse. Far in the west Cornwall and Devon rose; and in the east the men of Norfolk captured Norwich and established a "commonwealth" on Mousehold Hill, where Robert Ket, albeit himself a landlord of ancient family, laid down the law, and no rich man did what he liked with his own. The civil war, which the French king had hoped to evoke from Seymour's conspiracy, seemed to have come at last, and with it the opportunity of France. On August 8, 1549, at Whitehall Palace, the French ambassador made a formal declaration of war.

The successful Chauvinist policy of the French government would have precipitated a conflict long before but for the efforts of the English to avoid it. Henry II had begun his reign by breaking off the negotiations for an alliance with England, and declining to ratify the arrangement which the English and French commissioners had drawn up for the delimitation of the Boulonnais. But a variety of circumstances induced him to modify for a time his martial ardour, and restrict his hostility to a policy of pin-pricks administered to the English in their French possessions. The complete defeat of the German Princes at Mühlberg (April, 1547) made Henry anxious as to the direction in which the Emperor would turn his victorious arms; and the rout of the Scots at Pinkie five months later inspired a wholesome respect for English power. Then, in 1548, Guienne broke out in revolt against the *gabelle*, and clamoured for the privileges it had once enjoyed under its English kings. Charles V, moreover, although he disliked the religious changes in England and declined to take any active part against the Scots, gave the French to understand that he considered the Scots his enemies. Somerset, meanwhile, did his best to keep on friendly terms with Charles, and sought to mitigate his dislike of the First Act of Uniformity by granting the Princess Mary a dispensation to hear mass in private. Unless the Emperor's attention was absorbed elsewhere, a French attack on England might provoke an imperial onslaught on France.

Still, the endless bickerings with France about Boulogne were very exasperating; and eventually the Protector offered to restore it at once for the sum stipulated in the treaty of 1546, if France would further the marriage between Edward VI and Mary, Queen of Scots. That, however, was the last thing to which the Guises would consent; the preservation of their influence in Scotland was at that moment the mainspring of their action and the chief cause of the quarrel with England. The only condition on which they would keep the peace was the abandonment of Scotland to their designs, and that condition the Protector refused to the last to grant. Before the end of June, 1549, the French had assumed so threatening an attitude that Somerset sent Paget to Charles V with proposals for the marriage of the Princess Mary with the Infante John of Portugal, for the delivery of Boulogne into the Emperor's hands, and for a joint invasion of France by Imperial and English armies. This embassy seems to have alarmed Henry II, and he at once appointed commissioners to settle the disputes in the Boulonnais. The Protector thereupon forbade Paget to proceed with the negotiations for a joint invasion. The Emperor at the same time, doubtful of the value of England's alliance in her present disturbed condition, and immersed in anxieties of his own, declined to undertake the burden of Boulogne, or to knit any closer his ties with England. This refusal encouraged the French king to begin hostilities. He had collected an army on the borders of the Boulonnais; and in August it crossed the frontier. Ambleteuse (Newhaven) was captured through treachery; Blackness was taken by assault; Boulogneberg was dismantled and abandoned by the English; and the French forces sat down to besiege Boulogne.

The success of the French was mainly due to England's domestic troubles. Levies which had been raised for service in France were diverted to Devon or Norfolk. Fortunately, both these revolts were crushed before the war with France had lasted a fortnight. The rising in the west, for which religion had furnished a pretext and enclosures the material, died away after the fight at the Barns of Crediton, and the relief of Exeter by Russell on August 9. The eastern rebels, who were stirred solely by social grievances, caused more alarm; and a suspicion lest the Princess Mary should be at their back gave some of the Council sleepless nights. The Marquis of Northampton was driven out of Norwich, and the restraint and orderliness of the rebels' proceedings secured them a good deal of sympathy in East Anglia. Warwick, however, to whom the command was now entrusted, was a soldier of real ability, and with the help of Italian and Spanish mercenaries he routed the insurgents on August 26 at the battle of Dussindale, near Mousehold Hill. His victory made Warwick the hero of the gentlemen of England. He had always opposed the Protector's agrarian schemes, and he was now in a position to profit by their failure.

The revolts had placed Somerset in a predicament from which a modern minister would have sought refuge in resignation. His sympathy with the insurgents weakened his action against them; and his readiness to pardon and reluctance to proscribe exasperated most of his colleagues. He was still obstinate in his assertion of the essential justice of the rebels' complaints, and was believed to be planning for the approaching meeting of Parliament more radical measures of redress than had yet been laid before it. Paget wrote in alarm lest far-reaching projects should be rashly adopted which required ten years' deliberation; and other officials made Cecil the recipient of fearful warnings against the designs of the "Commonwealth's men." The Council and the governing classes generally were in no mood for measures of conciliation, and disasters abroad and disorders at home afforded a good pretext for removing the man to whom it was convenient to ascribe them.

The malcontents found an excellent party-leader in Warwick; few men in English history have shown a greater capacity for subtle intrigue or smaller respect for principle. A brilliant soldier, a skilful diplomatist, and an accomplished man of the world, he was described at the time as the modern Alcibiades. No one could better turn to his own purposes the passions and interests of others, or throw away his tools with less compunction when they had served his end. Masking profound ambitions under the guise of the utmost deference to his colleagues, he never at the time of his greatest influence attempted to claim a position of formal superiority. Afterwards, when he was practically ruler of England, he sat only fourth in the order of precedence at the Council-board; and content with the substance of power, he eschewed such titles as Protector of the Realm or Governor of the King's person.

In the general feeling of discontent he had little difficulty in uniting various sections in an attack on the Protector. The public at large were put in mind of Somerset's ill-success abroad; the landed gentry needed no reminder of his attempts to check their enclosures. Protestant zealots recalled his slackness in dealing with Mass-priests, and Catholics hated his Prayer Book. Hopes were held out to all; Gardiner in the Tower expected his release; Bonner appealed against his deprivation; and Southampton made sure of being restored to the woolsack. Privy Councillors had private griefs as well as public grounds to allege; the Protector had usurped his position in defiance of Henry's will; he had neglected their advice and browbeaten them when they remonstrated; he consulted and enriched only his chosen friends; Somerset House was erected, but Warwick's parks were ploughed up.

It was at Warwick's and Southampton's houses in Holborn that the plot against the Protector was hatched in September, 1549; and the immediate excuse for his deposition appears to have been the abandonment, after a brave defence, of Haddington, the chief English stronghold in Scotland (September 14). Somerset had left Westminster on the 12th with the King and removed to Hampton Court; Cranmer, Paget, St John, the two Secretaries of State, Petre and Sir Thomas Smith, and the Protector's own Secretary, Cecil, remained with him till the beginning of October; but the rest of the Council secretly gathered in London and collected their retainers. The aldermen of the City were on their side, but the apprentices and poorer classes generally adhered to the Protector. One of Warwick's methods of enlisting the support of the army was to send their captains to Somerset with petitions for higher pay than he knew the Protector could grant. The Duke apparently suspected nothing, unless suspicion be traced in the "matter of importance" to which he referred in his letter of the 27th, urging Russell and Herbert to hasten their return from the west. But by the 3rd or 4th of October rumours of what was happening reached him. On the latter day that "crafty fox Shebna," as Knox called St John, deserted to his colleagues in London, and secured the Tower by displacing Somerset's friends. On the 6th Somerset sent Petre to demand an explanation of the Council's conduct; but Petre did not return.

The Protector now thought of raising the masses against the classes. Handbills were distributed inciting the commons to rise in his defence; extortioners and "great masters" were conspiring, they were told, against the Protector because he had procured the peasants their pardon. On the night of the 6th he hurried the King to Windsor for the sake of greater security. But either he repented of his efforts to stir a social war, or he saw that they would be futile; for in a letter to the Council on the 7th he offered to submit upon reasonable conditions drawn up by representatives of both parties. The Council in London delayed their answer until they had heard from Russell and Herbert, to whom both parties had appealed for help. The commanders of the western army were at Wilton, and their action would decide the issue of peace or war. They promptly strengthened their forces, and moved up to Andover. There they found the country in a general uproar; five or six thousand men from the neighbouring counties were preparing to march to Somerset's aid. But Russell and Herbert were disgusted with the Protector's inflammatory appeals to the turbulent commons; they threw the whole weight of their influence on the Council's side, and succeeded in quieting the commotion, reporting their measures to both the rival factions.

On receipt of this intelligence the Lords in London brushed aside the conciliatory pleas of the King, Cranmer, Paget, and Smith, and took steps to effect the Protector's arrest. They were aided by treacherous advice from Paget, who purchased his own immunity at the expense of his colleagues. In accordance probably with Paget's suggestions, Sir Philip Hoby was sent to Windsor on the 10th with solemn promises from the

Council that the Duke should suffer no loss in lands, goods, or honours, and that his adherents should not be deprived of their offices. On the delivery of this message Paget fell on his knees before the Protector, and, with tears in his eyes, besought him to avail himself of the Council's merciful disposition. The others, relieved of their apprehensions, wept for joy and counselled submission. Somerset then gave way; and, through the "diligent travail" of Cranmer and Paget, his servants were removed from attendance on the King's person. When this measure had been effected, the Council no longer considered itself bound to observe the promises by which it had induced the Protector and his adherents to submit. Wingfield, St Leger, and Williams were sent with an armed force to arrest them all except Cranmer and Paget. On the 12th the whole Council went down to Windsor to complete the revolution. Somerset was conveyed to London, paraded as a prisoner through the streets, and shut up in the Tower; Smith was deprived of the secretaryship, expelled from the Council, and also sent to the Tower; and a like fate befell the rest of those who had remained faithful to the Protector. Of the victors, Warwick resumed the office of Lord High Admiral, which had been vacant since Seymour's attainder; Dr Nicholas Wotton, who was also Dean of Canterbury and of York, succeeded Smith as Secretary; and Paget received a peerage in reward for his services. The distribution of the more important offices was deferred until it was settled which section of the Protector's opponents was to have the upper hand in the new government. For the present it was advisable to meet Parliament with as united a front as possible, in order to secure its sanction for the Protector's deposition, and its reversal of so much of his policy as both sections agreed in detesting.

On the broader aspects of that policy there was not much difference of opinion. Most people of influence distrusted that liberty on which Somerset set so much store. Sir John Mason, for instance, an able and educated politician, described his repeal of Henry VIII's laws concerning verbal treason as the worst act done in that generation; and in accordance with this view a bill was introduced declaring it felony to preach and hold "divers" opinions. Differences about the definition of the offence apparently caused this bill to fail; but measures sufficiently drastic were passed to stifle any opposition to the new government. Ministers sought to perpetuate their tenure of office by making it high treason for anyone to attempt to turn them out. That tremendous penalty, the heaviest known to the law, had hitherto been reserved for offences against the sacrosanct persons of royalty; it was now employed to protect those who wielded royal authority. It became high treason for twelve or more persons to meet with the object of killing or even imprisoning a member of the Privy Council—an unparalleled enactment which, had it been retrospective, would have rendered the Privy Council itself liable to a charge of treason for its action against the Protector. The same clause imposed the same penalty upon persons assembling for the purpose of "altering the laws"; and the Act also omitted the safeguards Somerset had provided against the abuse of such treason laws as he had left on the Statute-book; it contained no clause limiting the time within which charges of treason were to be preferred or requiring the evidence of two witnesses.

The fact that this Act did not pass until it had been read six times in the Commons and six times in the Lords may indicate that it encountered considerable opposition; but there was probably little hesitation in reversing the Protector's agrarian policy. Parliament was not indeed content with that; it met (November 4, 1549) in a spirit of exasperation and revenge, and it went back, not only upon the radical proposals of Somerset, but also upon the whole tenour of Tudor land legislation. Enclosures had been forbidden again and again; they were now expressly declared to be legal; and Parliament enacted that lords of the manor might "approve themselves of their wastes, woods, and pastures notwithstanding the gainsaying and contradiction of their tenants." In order that the process might be without let or hindrance, it was made treason for forty, and felony for twelve, persons to meet for the purpose of breaking down any enclosure or enforcing any right of way; to summon such an assembly or incite to such an act was also felony; and any copyholder refusing to help in repressing it forfeited his copyhold for life. The same penalty was attached to hunting in any enclosure and to assembling with the object of abating rents or the price of corn; but the prohibition against capitalists conspiring to raise prices was repealed, and so were the taxes which Somerset had imposed on sheep and woollen cloths. The masses had risen against the classes, and the classes took their revenge.

This, however, was not the kind of reaction most desired by the Catholics who, led by Southampton, had assisted Warwick to overthrow Somerset. Southampton was moved by private grudges, but he also desired a return to Catholic usages or at least a pause in the process of change; and for a time it seemed that his party might prevail. "Those cruel beasts, the Romanists," wrote one evangelical divine, were already beginning to triumph, to revive the Mass, and to threaten faithful servants of Christ with the fate of the fallen Duke. They were, said another, struggling earnestly for their kingdom, and even Parliament felt it necessary to denounce rumours that the old Latin service and superstitious uses would be restored. Southampton was one of the six lords to whose charge the person of the King was specially entrusted; the Earl of Arundel was another, and Southwell reappeared at the Council board. Bonner had been deprived by Cranmer in September; but no steps were taken to find a successor, and the decision might yet be reversed. Gardiner petitioned for release, while Hooper thought himself in the greatest peril.

So the balance trembled. But Southampton was no match for "that most faithful and intrepid soldier of Christ," as Hooper styled Warwick. "England," he went on, "cannot do without him." Neither could the Earl afford to discard such zealous adherents as the Reformers; in them he found his main support. They compared him with Moses and Joshua, and described him and Dorset as "the two most shining lights of the Church of England." They believed that Somerset had been deposed for his slackness in the cause of religious persecution; Warwick resolved to run no such risk. The tendency towards religious change, which Henry VIII had failed to stop, was still strong, and Warwick threw himself into the stream. Privately he seems, if he believed in anything, to have favoured Catholic doctrines; and the consciousness of his insincerity made him all the louder in his professions of Protestant zeal, and all the more eager to push to extremes the principles of the Reformers. He became, in Hooper's words, "a most holy and fearless instrument of the Word of God."

But this policy could not be combined with the conciliation of Catholics; and the coalition which had driven Somerset from power fell asunder, as soon as its immediate object had been achieved, and it was called upon to formulate a policy of its own. Southampton ceased to attend the Council after October; and Parliament, which had completely reversed the Protector's liberal and social programme, effected almost as great a change in the methods and aims of his religious policy. The direction may have been the same, but it is pure assumption to suppose that the Protector would have gone so far as his successors or employed the same violence to attain his ends. The difference in character between the two administrators was vividly illustrated in the session of Parliament which began a month after the change. Under Somerset there had always been a good attendance of Bishops, and a majority of them had voted for all his religious proposals; at the opening of the first session after his fall there were only nine Bishops, and a majority of them voted against two of the three measures of ecclesiastical importance passed during its course. One was the Act for the destruction of all service books other than the Book of Common Prayer and Henry's Primer; and the other was a renewal of the provision for the reform of Canon Law. A majority of Bishops voted for the bill appointing a commission to draw up a new Ordinal; but, when they complained that their jurisdiction was despised and drafted a bill for its restoration, the measure was rejected.

The prorogation of Parliament (February, 1550) was followed by the final overthrow of the Catholic party and the complete establishment of Warwick's control over the government. He had already begun to pack the Council, which had remained practically unchanged since Henry's death, by adding to it five of his own adherents. Southampton was now expelled from the Council, Arundel was deprived of his office of Lord Chamberlain, and Southwell was sent to the Tower. The offices vacated by the Catholic lords and Somerset's party were distributed among Warwick's friends. St John became Earl of Wiltshire and Lord High Treasurer; Warwick succeeded him as Lord Great Master of the Household and President of the Council; and Northampton succeeded Warwick as Great Chamberlain of England. Arundel's office of Chamberlain of the Household was conferred on Wentworth, and Paget's Comptrollership on Wingfield; Russell was created Earl of Bedford, and Herbert was made President of the Council of Wales.

The new government now felt firm in the saddle, and it proceeded to turn its attention to foreign affairs. His failure abroad had been the chief ostensible reason for Somerset's downfall; but his successors had done nothing to redeem their implied promise of amendment. In spite of the fact that the agrarian insurrections—the immediate cause of the Protector's reverses in France and Scotland—had been suppressed, and large bodies of troops thus set free for service elsewhere, not a place had been recaptured in France, and in Scotland nearly all the English strongholds fell during the winter into the enemy's hands. The Council preferred peace to an attempt to retrieve their fortunes by war; and early in 1550 Warwick made secret overtures to Henry II. The French pushed their advantage to the uttermost; and the peace concluded in March was the most ignominious treaty signed by England during the century.

Boulogne, which was to have been restored four years later for 800,000 crowns, was surrendered for half that sum. All English strongholds in Scotland were to be given up without compensation; England bound itself to make no war on that country unless fresh grounds of offence were given, and condoned the marriage of Mary to the Dauphin of France. The net result was the abandonment of the whole Tudor policy towards Scotland, the destruction of English influence across the Border, and the establishment of French control in Edinburgh. Henry II began to speak of himself as King of Scotland; it was as much subject to him, he said, as France itself; and he boasted that by this peace he had now added to these two realms a third, namely England, of whose King, subjects, and resources he had such absolute disposal that the three might be reckoned as one kingdom of which he was King. To make himself yet more secure, he began a policy of active, though secret, intervention in Ireland. Had he succeeded in this, he would really have held England in the hollow of his hand; had a son been born to Mary Stewart and Francis II, England might even have become a French province. Fortunately, the accession of Mary Tudor broke the French ring which girt England round about; but it was certainly not Warwick's merit that England was delivered from perhaps the most pressing foreign danger with which she was ever threatened.

While, however, the policy which Warwick adopted involved a reversal of the time-honoured Burgundian alliance and a criminal neglect of England's ultimate interests, its immediate effects were undeniably advantageous to the government. It was at once relieved from the pressure of war on two fronts, and an intolerable drain on the exchequer was stopped. Security from foreign interference afforded an excuse for reducing expenditure on armaments and military forces, and even for seriously impairing the effective strength of the navy, the creation of which had been Henry VIII's least questionable achievement; and the Council was left free to pursue its religious policy, even to the persecution of the Princess Mary, without fear of interruption from her cousin the Emperor. The alliance of England, Scotland, and France was a combination which Charles could not afford to attack, more particularly when the league between Henry II, Maurice of Saxony, and the reviving Protestant Princes in Germany gave him more than enough to do to defend himself. France, the persecutor of heresy at home, lent her support to the English government while it pursued its campaign against Roman doctrine, just as she had countenanced Henry VIII while he was uprooting the Roman jurisdiction.

The path of the government was thus made easy abroad; but at home it was crowded with difficulties. The diversity of religious opinion, which Henry VIII's severity had only checked and Somerset's lenience had encouraged, grew ever more marked. The New Learning was, in the absence of effective opposition, carrying all before it in the large cities; and the more trenchantly a preacher denounced the old doctrines, the greater were the crowds which gathered to hear him. The favourite divine in London was Hooper, who went far beyond anything which the Council had yet done or at present intended. Between twenty and thirty editions of the Bible had appeared since the beginning of the reign, and nearly all were made vehicles, by their annotations, of attacks on Catholic dogma. Altars, images, painted glass windows became the object of a popular violence which the Council was unable, even if it was willing, to restrain; and the parochial clergy indulged in a ritual lawlessness which the Bishops encouraged or checked according to their own individual preferences. That the majority of the nation disliked both these changes and their method may perhaps be assumed, but the men of the Old Learning made little stand against the men of the New. In a revolution the first advantage generally lies with the aggressors. The Catholics had not been rallied, nor the Counter-Reformation organised, and their natural leaders had been silenced for their opposition to the government. But there were deeper causes at work; the Catholic Church had latterly denied to the laity any voice in the determination of Catholic doctrine; but now the laity had been called in to decide. Discussion had descended from Court and from senate into the street, where only one of the parties was adequately equipped for the contest. Catholics still were content to do as they had been taught and to leave the matter to the clergy; they were ill fitted to cope with antagonists who regarded theology as a matter for private judgment, and had by study of the Scriptures to some extent prepared themselves for its exercise. The authority of the Church, to which Catholics bowed, had suffered many rude shocks; and in the appeal to the Scriptures they were no match for the zeal and conviction of their opponents.

Under the circumstances it might seem that the Council would have done well to resort to some of Henry VIII's methods for enforcing uniformity; and indeed both parties agreed in demanding greater rigour. But they could not agree on the question to whom the rigour should be applied; their contentions indirectly tended towards the emancipation of conscience from the control of authority, though such a solution seemed shocking alike to those who believed in the Royal and to those who believed in the Papal Supremacy. There was no course open to the government that would have satisfied all contemporary or modern critics. England was in the throes of a revolution in which no government could have maintained perfect order or avoided all persecution. The Council's policy lacked the extreme moderation and humanity of Somerset's rule, but it averted open disruption, and did so at the cost of less rigour than characterised the rule of Henry VIII, of Mary, or of Elizabeth.

At one end of the religious scale Joan Bocher, whom Somerset had left in prison after her condemnation by the ecclesiastical Courts in the hope that she might be converted, was burnt in May, 1550; and a year later another heretic, George van Paris, suffered a similar fate. Against Roman Catholics the penalties of the first Act of Uniformity now began to be enforced; but they were limited to clerical offenders and of these there seem to have been comparatively few. Dr Cole was expelled from the Wardenship of New College, and Dr Morwen, President of Corpus Christi, Oxford, was sent for a time to the Fleet; two divines, Crispin and Moreman, who had been implicated in the Cornish rebellion, were confined in the Tower; two of Gardiner's chaplains, Seton and Watson, are said to have been subjected to some restraint; four others, John Boxall, afterwards Queen Mary's Secretary, William Rastell, More's nephew, Nicholas Harpsfield and Dr Richard Smith, whose recantations were as numerous as his apologies for the Catholic faith, fled to Flanders; and these, with Cardinal Pole, whose attainder was not reversed, make up the list of those who are said by Roman martyrologists to have suffered for their belief in the reign of Edward VI. To them, however, must be added five or six Bishops, who were deposed. Bonner was the only Bishop deprived in 1550, but in the following year Gardiner, Heath of Worcester, Day of Chichester, and Voysey of Exeter all vacated their sees, and Tunstall of Durham was sent to the Tower. Their places were filled with zealous Reformers; Coverdale became Bishop of Exeter, Ridley succeeded Bonner at London, and Ponet took Ridley's see; Ponet was soon transferred to Gardiner's seat at Winchester, and Scory supplied the place left vacant by Ponet, but was almost at once translated to Day's bishopric at Chichester. Warwick wished to enthrone John Knox at Rochester as a whetstone to Cranmer, but the Scottish Reformer proved ungrateful; and Rochester, which had seen five Bishops in as many years, remained vacant to the end of the reign.

The most remarkable of these creations and translations, which were made by letters patent, was perhaps the elevation of Hooper to the see of Gloucester. Hooper had, after a course of Zwinglian theology at Zurich, become chaplain to the Protector on the eve of his fall; but he found a more powerful friend in Warwick, who made him Lent preacher at Court in February, 1550. He was one of those zealous and guileless Reformers in whom Warwick found his choicest instruments; he combined fervent denunciations of the evils of the times with extravagant admiration for the man in whom they were most strikingly personified; and, as soon as his Lenten sermons were finished, he was offered the See of Gloucester. He declined it from scruples about the new Ordinal, the oath invoking the Saints, and the episcopal vestments. After a nine months' controversy, in which the whole bench of Bishops, with Bucer and Martyr, were arrayed against him and only John à Lasco and Micronius appeared on his side, and after some weeks' confinement in the Fleet, Hooper allowed himself to be consecrated. The simultaneous vacancy of Worcester enabled the Council to sweep away one of Henry VIII's new bishoprics by uniting it with Gloucester; and another was abolished by the translation of Thirlby from Westminster to Norwich, and the reunion of the former see with London.

These episcopal changes afforded scope for another sort of ecclesiastical spoliation; most of the new Bishops were compelled to alienate some of their manors to courtiers as the price of their elevation; and Ponet went so far as to surrender all his lands in return for a fixed stipend of two thousand marks. These lands were for the most part distributed among Warwick's adherents; and no small portion of the chantry endowments and much Church plate found its way to the same destination. Somerset had issued a commission in 1547 for taking a general inventory of Church goods in order to prevent the private embezzling which was so common just before and during the course of the Reformation; and this measure was supplemented by various orders to particular persons or corporations to restore such plate and ornaments as they had appropriated. But it may be doubted whether these prohibitions were very effectual; and after Somerset's fall private and public spoliation went on rapidly until it culminated (March, 1551) in a comprehensive seizure by the government of all such Church plate as remained unappropriated.

The confiscation of chantry lands followed a similar course. The first charge upon them was the support of the displaced chantry priests, whose pensions in 1549 amounted to a sum equivalent to between two and three hundred thousand pounds in modern currency. The next was stated to be "the erecting of Grammar schools to the education of youth in virtue and godliness, the further augmenting of the Universities, and better provision for the poor and needy." But the bill introduced into Parliament in 1549 "for the making of schools" failed to pass the House of Lords; and the "further order" designed by the Protector was inevitably postponed. Meanwhile the confiscated chantry lands afforded tempting facilities for the satisfaction of the King's immediate needs. In 1548-9 some five thousand pounds' worth were sold and the proceeds devoted to the defence of the realm. But less legitimate practices soon obtained; the chantry lands were regarded as the last dish in the last course of the feast provided by the wealth of the Church, and the importunity of courtiers correspondingly increased. Grants as well as sales became common; the recipients, with few exceptions, repudiated the obligation to provide for schools out of their newly-won lands; and the fortunes of many private families were raised on funds intended for national education. A few schools were founded by private benefactors, and it is probable that education gained on the whole by its emancipation from the control of the Church. But it was not until the closing years of the reign that the government made a serious endeavour to secure the adequate maintenance of those schools whose foundations had been shaken by the abolition of chantries; and Edward VI's services to education consisted principally in assigning a fixed annual pension to schools whose endowments of much greater potential value had been appropriated.

These proceedings, like the other religious changes made during 1550 and 1551, were effected by the action of the Council, of individual Bishops, or of private persons; for Parliament, which Warwick distrusted, did not meet between February, 1550, and January, 1552. But some of the Council's measures were based upon legislation passed in the session of 1549-50; such were the wholesale destruction of old service-books which wrought particular havoc among the libraries of Oxford and Cambridge, and the compilation and execution of the new Ordinal, which was published in March and brought into use in April, 1550. By it a number of ceremonies hitherto used at ordinations were discontinued; and it embodied a clause which has been divergently interpreted both as abolishing and as retaining all the minor orders beneath that of deacon. Ridley signalised his elevation to the see of London by a severe visitation of his diocese, and by reducing the altars in St Paul's and elsewhere to the status and estimation of "the Lord's tables." Corpus Christi Day and many Saints' days ceased to be observed partly because they savoured of popery, and partly because the cessation of work impeded the acquisition of wealth. Cranmer, Bucer, and Martyr were secretly busy revising the Prayer-Book, and the Council was engaged in an attempt to force the Princess Mary to relinquish her private masses, when suddenly in the autumn of 1551 the nation was startled by the news of another Court revolution.

Somerset, after his submission and deposition from the Protectorate, had been released from the Tower on February 6, 1550. In April he was readmitted to the Privy Council; and in May he was made a gentleman of the privy chamber and received back such of his lands as had not already been sold. The Duke's easy-going nature induced him readily to forgive the indignities he had suffered at Warwick's hands; and in June, 1550, the reconciliation went so far that a marriage was concluded between the Duke's daughter and Warwick's eldest son, Lord Lisle. From this time Somerset, to all appearance, took an active part in the government. But it was clear that he only existed on sufferance, as a dependant of the Earl of Warwick. The situation was too galling to last long. The Duke was allowed no free access to his royal nephew; he was excluded from the innermost secrets of the ruling faction, and was often dependent for knowledge of the government's plans on such information as he could extract from attendants on the King; he was not only opposed to almost every principle on which Warwick acted, but was personally an obstacle to the achievement of the designs which the Earl was beginning to cherish. He was thus, unless he was willing to be Warwick's tool, forced to become the centre of active or passive resistance—the leader of the opposition, in so far as Tudor practice tolerated such a personage. Within three months of his readmission to the Council he was exerting himself to procure the release of Gardiner, of the Earl of Arundel, and of other prisoners in the Tower; and, while Warwick was absent, Somerset was strong enough to obtain the Council's promotion or restoration of several of his adherents. He attempted to prevent the withdrawal of the Princess Mary's licence to hear mass, and sought so far as he could to restore a friendly feeling between England and the Emperor. In these efforts he found considerable support among the moderate party; and the spiritless conduct of foreign affairs by the new government, coupled with the harshness of its domestic administration, made many regret the Protector's deposition. Before the session of 1549–50 broke up, a movement was initiated for his restoration; the project was defeated by a prorogation, but it was resolved to renew it as soon as Parliament met again, and this was one of the reasons why Parliament was not summoned till after Somerset's death.

Warwick viewed the Duke's conduct with anger, which increased as his own growing unpopularity made Somerset appear more and more formidable; and before the end of September, 1551, Warwick had elaborated a comprehensive scheme for the further advancement of himself and his faction and for the total ruin of Somerset and the opposition. Cecil, the ablest of the ex-Protector's friends, had ingratiated himself with Warwick by his zeal against Gardiner at the time when Somerset was endeavouring to procure his release, and in September, 1550, he had been sworn one of the two Secretaries of State; a year later (October 4, 1551) he occurs among the list of Warwick's supporters marked out for promotion. Warwick himself was created Duke of Northumberland; Grey, Marquis of Dorset, became Duke of Suffolk; Wiltshire Marquis of Winchester; Herbert Earl of Pembroke; while knighthoods were bestowed on Cecil, Sidney (Warwick's son-in-law), Henry Dudley (his kinsman), and Henry Neville. On the 16th Somerset and his friends, including Lord Grey de Wilton, the Earl of Arundel, and a dozen others, were arrested and sent to the Tower; Paget had been sequestered a fortnight earlier, to get him out of the way.

The real cause and occasion of this sudden *coup d'état* are still obscure. It is probable that foreign affairs had more to do with the matter than appears on the surface. The Constable of France, when informed of it, suggested that Charles V and the Princess Mary were probably at Somerset's back, and offered to send French troops to Northumberland's aid; it is quite as likely that Henry II was at the bottom of Northumberland's action. Somerset had, since the days when he served in the Emperor's suite, been an imperialist; and Charles V, who still professed a personal friendship for him, would have welcomed his return to power in place of the Francophil administration, which had just (June, 1551) put the seal on its foreign policy by negotiating a marriage between Edward VI and Henry II's daughter, Elizabeth. The dispute with the Emperor concerning the treatment of the Princess Mary was at its height; and it is possible that plot and counterplot were in essence a struggle between French and Imperial influence in England. In any case the stories told to the young King and published abroad were obviously false; Edward was informed that his uncle had plotted the murder of Northumberland, Northampton, and Pembroke, the seizure of the Crown and other measures against himself, to which the young King's knowledge of the fate of Edward V would give a sinister interpretation; the people of London were informed that he meant to destroy the city.

The plot was said to have been hatched in April, 1551; but the first hint of its existence was conveyed to the government in a private conversation between Northumberland and Sir Thomas Palmer on October 4, long after the conspiracy, if it ever was real, had been abandoned. Palmer, who was one of the accomplices, was nevertheless left at liberty for a fortnight; he was never put upon his trial, and, when Somerset was finally disposed of, he became Northumberland's right-hand man; finally, he confessed before his death that his accusation had been invented at Northumberland's instigation. The Earl of Arundel, who, according to Northumberland's theory, had been the principal accomplice in Somerset's felony, was subsequently readmitted to the Council, became Lord Steward of the Household to Mary and to Elizabeth, and

Chancellor of the University of Oxford. Paget, at whose house the intended assassination was to have taken place, was never brought into Court; neither was Lord Grey, another accomplice, who was afterwards made captain of Guines "as amends" for the unjust charge. To the minor conspirators a very simple principle was applied quite irrespective of their guilt: if they implicated Somerset, they were released without trial; if they persisted in asserting their own and his innocence they were executed. But, in spite of all Northumberland's efforts, no confirmation was obtained of Palmer's main charge. Scores of witnesses were imprisoned in the Tower and put to torture; but the story of the intended assassination was so baseless that the charge did not appear in any one of the five indictments returned against Somerset, and was not so much as alluded to in the examinations of the Duke himself and his chief adherents.

Meanwhile, stringent measures were taken to prevent disturbance. The creation of Lords-Lieutenant put local administration and the local militia into the hands of Northumberland's friends, and provided him with an instrument akin to Cromwell's Major-generals. London was overawed by the newly-organised bands of *gens d'armes*; and an effort was made to appease one source of dissatisfaction by proclaiming a new and purified coinage. Parliament, which was to have met in November, was further prorogued; and Northumberland's control of the government was strengthened by a decision that the King's order (he was just fourteen) should be absolutely valid without the countersignature of a single member of the Council. Lord-Chancellor Rich resigned soon after in alarm at this violent measure, and he consequently took no part in Somerset's trial. The tribunal consisted of twenty-six out of forty-seven peers; among them were Northumberland, Northampton, and Pembroke, who were really parties in the case. They had already acted practically as accusers, had drawn up the charges, and examined the witnesses; they now assumed the function of judges, and after their verdict determined whether it should be executed or not.

The trial took place on December 1 at Westminster Hall; the charges were practically two, one of treason in conspiring to imprison a Privy Councillor, and one of felony in inciting to an unlawful assembly. Both these offences depended upon the atrocious statute which, passed in the panic of reaction after Somerset's fall, was to expire with the next session of Parliament—a further reason for its prorogation. In another respect the trial would not have been possible under any other Act; for that Act removed the previous limitation of thirty days within which accusations must be preferred, and five months had elapsed between Somerset's alleged offences and Palmer's accusation. Nevertheless the charge of treason broke down, and the government boasted of its magnanimity in condemning the prisoner to death only for felony. There was as little evidence for that offence as for the other, and the

1552] *Execution of Somerset.—Second Act of Uniformity.*   34

sum of the ex-Protector's guilt appears to have been this: he had spoken to one or two friends of the advisability of arresting Northumberland, Northampton, and Pembroke, calling a Parliament, and demanding an account of their evil government.

Somerset was sent back to the Tower amid extravagant demonstrations of joy by the people, who thought he had been acquitted. He remained there seven weeks, and there was a general expectation that no further steps would be taken against him. Parliament, however, was to meet on January 23, and it was certain that a movement in Somerset's favour would be made. Northumberland had endeavoured to strengthen his faction in the Commons by forcing his nominees on vacant constituencies; but his hold on Parliament remained nevertheless weaker than that of his rival, and it was therefore determined to get rid of Somerset once and for all. An order of the King drawn up on January 18 for the trial of Somerset's accomplices, was, before its submission to the Council on the following day, transformed by erasures and interlineations into an order for the Duke's execution. No record of the proceedings was entered in the Council's register; but Cecil, with a view to future contingencies, secured the King's memorandum and inscribed on the back of it the names of the Councillors who were present. Somerset's execution took place at sunrise on the 22nd; in spite of elaborate precautions a riot nearly broke out, but the Duke made no effort to turn to account the popular sympathy. He had resigned himself to his fate, and died with exemplary courage and dignity.

Parliament met on the following day, and it soon proved that Northumberland had been wise in his generation. Parliament could not restore Somerset to life, but it could at least ensure that no one should again be condemned by similar methods. It rejected a new treason bill designed to supply the place of the former expiring Act, and passed another providing that accusations must be made within three months of the offence, and that the prisoner must be confronted with two witnesses to his crime. The House of Commons also refused to pass a bill of attainder against Tunstall, Bishop of Durham, who had been imprisoned on a vague charge remotely connected with Somerset's pretended plots. His bishopric was, however, marked out for spoliation, and a few months later Tunstall was deprived by a civil Court. Parliament was more complaisant in religious matters, and passed the Second Act of Uniformity, besides another Act removing from the marriage of priests the stigma hitherto attaching to the practice as being only a licensed evil. The Second Act of Uniformity extended the scope of religious persecution by imposing penalties for recusancy upon laymen; if they neglected to attend common prayer on Sundays and holidays, they were to be subject to ecclesiastical censures and excommunication; if they attended any but the authorised form of worship, they were liable to six months' imprisonment for the first offence, a year's imprisonment for the second, and lifelong imprisonment for the third.

This Second Act of Uniformity also imposed a Second Book of Common Prayer. The First Book of Common Prayer had scarcely received the sanction of Parliament in 1549, when it began to be attacked as a halting makeshift by the Reformers. The fact that Gardiner expressed a modified approval of it was enough to condemn it in their eyes, and in the Second Book those parts which had won Gardiner's approval were carefully eliminated or revised. The Prayer Book of 1549 was elaborately examined by Bucer and more superficially by Peter Martyr; but the changes actually made were rather on lines indicated by Cranmer in his controversy with Gardiner than on those suggested by Bucer; and the actual revision was done by the Archbishop, assisted at times by Ridley. There is no proof that Convocation was consulted in the matter, nor is there any evidence that the Book underwent modification in its passage through Parliament. The net result was to minimise the possibility of such Catholic interpretations as had been placed on the earlier Book; in particular the Communion Office was radically altered until it approached very nearly to the Zwinglian idea of a commemorative rite. The celebrated Black Rubric, explaining away the significance of the ceremony of kneeling at Communion, was inserted on the Council's authority after the Act had been passed by Parliament. Two other ecclesiastical measures of importance were the *Reformatio legum ecclesiasticarum* and the compilation of the Forty-two Articles. The Articles of Religion, originally drawn up by Cranmer, were revised at the Council's direction and did not receive the royal signature until June, 1553, while Parliament in the same year refused its sanction to the Book of Canon Law prepared by the commissioners; lay objections to spiritual jurisdiction were the same, whether it was exercised by Catholic or by Protestant prelates.

The extensive reduction of Church ritual effected by the Second Act of Uniformity rendered superfluous a large quantity of Church property, and for its seizure by the Crown the government's financial embarrassments supplied an obvious motive. The subsidies granted in 1549-50, the money paid for the restitution of Boulogne, profits made by the debasement of the coinage, and other sources, had enabled Northumberland to tide over the Parliament of 1552, without demanding from it any further financial aid. But these sources were now exhausted, and in the ensuing summer the final gleanings from the Church were gathered in. Such chantry lands as had not been sold or granted away were now disposed of; all unnecessary church ornaments were appropriated; the lands of the dissolved bishoprics and attainted conspirators were placed on the market; church bells were taken down, organs were removed, and lead was stripped off the roofs. When these means failed, the heroic measure was proposed of demanding an account from all Crown officers of moneys received during the last twenty years. Still there was a deficit; and in the winter Northumberland was reduced to appealing to Parliament.

By this time his government had become so unpopular that he shrank from meeting a really representative assembly, and had recourse to an expedient which has been misrepresented as the normal practice of Tudor times. There had already been isolated instances of the exercise of government influence to force particular candidates on constituencies; but the Parliament of March, 1553, was the only one in the sixteenth century that can fairly be described as nominated by the government; and Renard, when discussing the question of a Parliament in the following August, asked Charles V whether he thought it advisable to have a general Parliament or merely an assembly of "notables" summoned after the manner introduced by Northumberland. A circular appears to have been sent round ordering the electors to return the members nominated by the Council. Even this measure was not considered sufficient to ensure a properly subservient House of Commons; and at the same time eleven new boroughs returning twenty-two members were created, principally in Cornwall, where Crown influence was supreme. The process of packing had already been applied to the Privy Council, more than half of which, as it existed in 1553, had been nominated since Northumberland's accession to power. To this Parliament the Duke represented his financial needs as exclusively due to the maladministration of the Protector, who had been deposed three and a half years before; and a subsidy was granted which was not, however, to be paid for two years. Acts were also passed with a view to checking fiscal abuses; but Northumberland again met with some traces of independence in the Commons, and Parliament was dissolved on March 31, having sat for barely a month.

The ground was fast slipping from under Northumberland's feet, and the Nemesis which had long dogged his steps was drawing perceptibly nearer. Zimri had no peace, and from the time of Somerset's fall never a month passed without some symptom of popular discontent. In October, 1551, a rumour spread that a coinage was being minted at Dudley Castle stamped with Northumberland's badge, the bear and ragged staff, and in 1552 he was widely believed to be aiming at the Crown. Even some of his favourite preachers began to denounce him in thinly veiled terms from the pulpit. No longer a Moses or Joshua, he was not obscurely likened to Ahitophel. His only support was the young King, over whose mind he had established complete dominion; and Edward VI was now slowly dying before his eyes. The consequences to himself of a demise of the Crown were only too clear; his ambition had led him into so many crimes and had made him so many enemies that his life was secure only so long as he controlled the government and prevented the administration of justice. There was no room for repentance; he could expect no mercy when his foes were once in a position to bring him to book. The accession of Mary would almost inevitably be followed by his own attainder; and the prospect drove him to make one last desperate bid for life and for power.

There were other temptations which led him to stake his all on a single throw. No immediate interference need be feared from abroad. Scotland, now little more than a province of France, had no desire to see a half-Spanish princess on the English throne, and France was even more reluctant to witness the transference of England's resources to the hands of Charles V. The Emperor was fully occupied with the French war, and Mary had nothing on which to rely except the temper of England. Northumberland's endeavour to alter the Succession might well seem worth the making. He could appeal to the fact that no woman had sat on the English throne, and that the only attempt to place one there had been followed by civil war. Margaret Beaufort had been excluded in favour of her son; and in the reign of Henry VIII there were not wanting those who preferred the claim of an illegitimate son to that of a legitimate daughter. He could also play upon the dread of religious reaction and of foreign domination which would ensue if Mary succeeded and, as she probably would, married an alien. The Netherlands, Hungary, and Bohemia had all by marriage been brought under Habsburg rule and with disastrous consequences; might not England be reserved for a similar fate? Some of these objections applied also to the Princess Elizabeth, but not all, and Northumberland would have stood a better chance of success had he selected as his candidate the daughter of Anne Boleyn. But such a solution would not necessarily have meant a continuance of his own supremacy, and that was the vital point.

Hence the Duke had recourse to a plan which was hopelessly illegal, illogical, unpopular, and unconstitutional. Edward VI was induced to settle the Crown on Lady Jane Grey, the grand-daughter of Henry VIII's sister, Mary, Duchess of Suffolk; she was married to Northumberland's fourth son, Guilford Dudley, and Dudley was to receive the Crown matrimonial, and thus mitigate the objections to a female sovereign. The arrangement was illegal, because Edward VI had not been empowered by law, as Henry had, to leave the Crown by will; and any attempt to alter the Succession established by Parliament and by Henry's will was treason. It was illogical, because, even supposing that Henry's will could be set aside and his two daughters excluded as illegitimate, the next claimant was Mary, Queen of Scots, the grand-daughter of Henry's elder sister Margaret. Moreover, if the Suffolk line was adopted, the proper heir was Lady Jane's mother, the wife of Henry Grey, Duke of Suffolk. There was thus little to recommend the King's "device" except the arbitrary will of Northumberland, who in May, 1553, endeavoured to implicate his chief supporters in the plot by a series of dynastic marriages. His daughter Catharine was given to Lord Hastings; Lady Jane's sister Catharine to Pembroke's son, Lord Herbert; and Lady Jane's cousin

Margaret Clifford (another possible claimant) to Northumberland's brother Andrew. The news of these arrangements confirmed the popular suspicions of the Duke's designs, and during the month of June foreign ambassadors in London were kept pretty well informed of the progress of the plot. The reluctant consent of the Council was obtained by a promise that Parliament should be summoned at once to confirm the settlement; and on June 11 the judges were ordered to draw up letters patent embodying the young King's wishes. They resisted at first, but Edward's urgent commands, Northumberland's violence, and a pardon under the Great Seal for their action at length extorted compliance. On the 21st the Council with some open protests and many mental reservations signed the letters patent. The Tower had been secured; troops had been hastily raised; and the fleet had been manned. Every precaution that fear could inspire had been taken when the last male Tudor died on July 6 at Greenwich; nothing remained but for the nation to declare, through such channels as were still left open, its verdict on the claims of Mary and the Duke of Northumberland's rule.

www.ingramcontent.com/pod-product-compliance
Lightning Source LLC
Chambersburg PA
CBHW061309040426
42444CB00010B/2570